Readers
LEVEL 2

Looking After Me

Going to

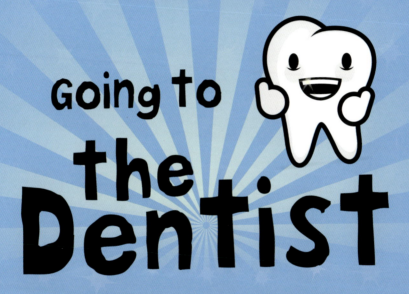

the Dentist

Sally Hewitt

This library edition published in 2015 by Quarto Library.,
an imprint of Quarto Publishing Group USA Inc.
3 Wrigley, Suite A
Irvine, CA 92618

Distributed in the United States and Canada by
Lerner Publisher Services
241 First Avenue North
Minneapolis, MN 55401 U.S.A.
www.lernerbooks.com

Library of Congress Cataloging-in-Publication Data

Hewitt, Sally, 1949- author.
 Going to the dentist / Sally Hewitt.
    pages cm. -- (Looking after me. Level 2)
 RK55.C5H49 2015
 617.6'45--dc23

                        2015010355

ISBN 978 1 93958 183 9

Printed in China

Picture credits
(t=top, b=bottom, l=left, r=right, c=center fc=front cover)

Shutterstock 4-5 Sergiy Bykhunenko, 6bl Robyn Mackenzie, 6-7 stavklem, 7 Yasonya, 8
wavebreakmedia, 20br donfiore, 22b Lusoimages, 22br Irina Rogova,
Steve Lumb 9, 10, 12, 13, 14-15, 17, 19, 20bl, 21, 22tl, 23

Words in **bold** can be found in the Glossary on page 24

Contents

Healthy Teeth

When you smile, people can see your teeth.

It's great if you have a nice smile with clean, healthy teeth.

5

Eating fruits and
vegetables is good
for your teeth.

"Chomp,
Chomp"

"Yum, Yum"

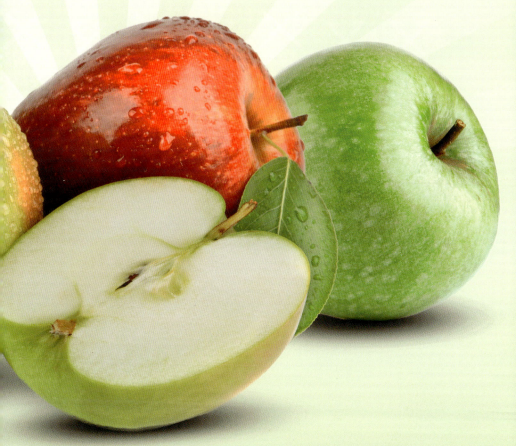

They help keep your teeth strong and healthy.

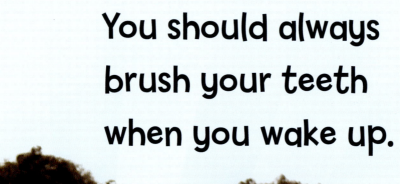

You should always brush your teeth when you wake up.

Brush them again when you go to bed or after you eat.

8

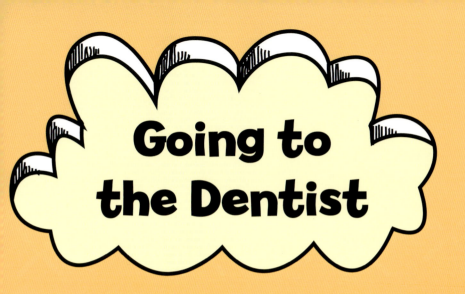

Going to the Dentist

The **dentist** will help you take care of your teeth.

You should visit the dentist twice a year.

9

The Waiting Room

10

If the dentist is busy, you will have to wait.

You can sit in the waiting room and look at a book.

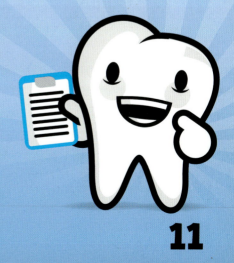

The Dentist's Chair

The dentist has a special chair for you to sit in. It moves up and down, and can lean back like a bed.

The dentist will give you special glasses to wear. They will **protect** your eyes.

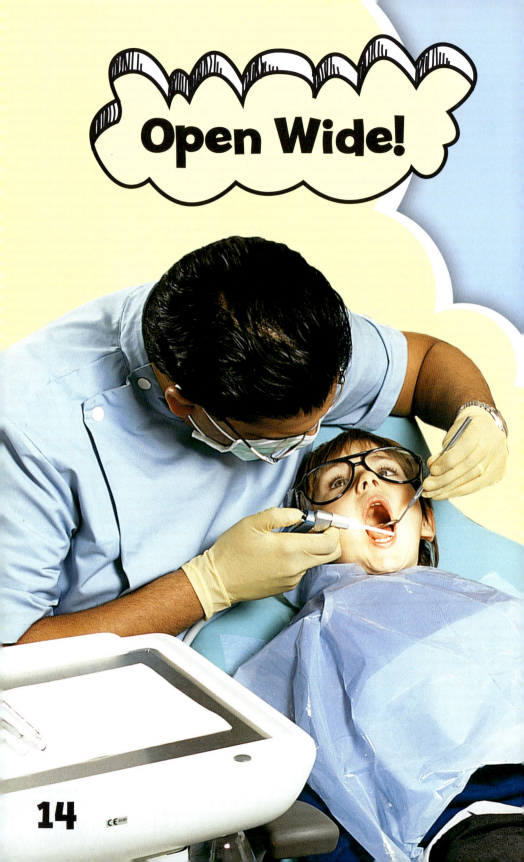

The dentist will ask
you to "open wide!"

The dentist will shine
a light into your mouth.
He will use a small mirror
to look at your teeth.

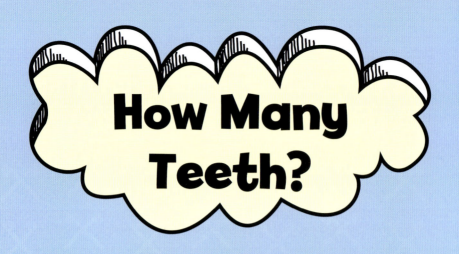

How Many Teeth?

The dentist will count your teeth.

Have all your **first teeth** grown? If so, you will have ten at the top of your mouth and ten at the bottom.

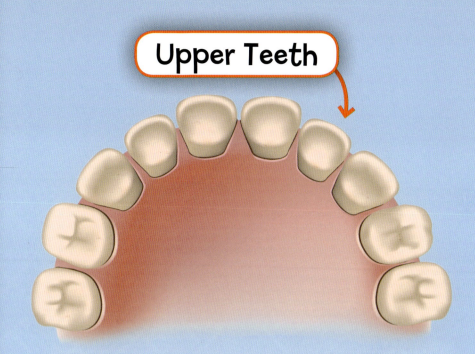

Upper Teeth

You will have twenty
teeth altogether!

Lower Teeth

Cleaning Teeth

The dentist will wash your teeth with water and clean them with tools.

The tools buzz as they clean and **polish** your teeth!

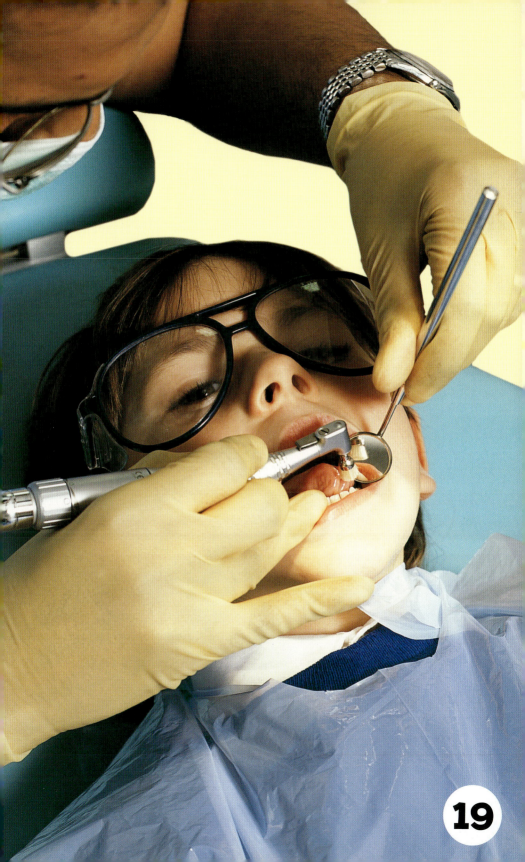

Afterwards, you can wash your mouth with water.

You can spit the water into the sink.

Keeping Teeth Clean

The dentist will show you the best way to brush your teeth.

Try to brush your teeth that way at home.

21

The dentist might give you a bag of things to help you keep your teeth clea

You might even get a sticker, too!

A Nice Smile

Do you have a younger brother or sister? You can show them how to brush their teeth.

Then they will have a nice smile as well.

23

Glossary

dentist   someone who knows a lot about teeth and helps you keep your teeth strong and healthy

first teeth   the teeth you grow as a baby—they are replaced by grown-up teeth that will last the rest of your life

polish   rub something to make it clean and shiny

protect   keep something safe